THE BLENDED FAMILY JOURNAL FOR TEENS

the

BLENDED FAMILY
Journal for Teens

PROMPTS AND PRACTICES FOR NAVIGATING
EMOTIONS AND FINDING YOUR WAY

DANIELLE SCHLAGEL

ROCKRIDGE
PRESS

Interior and Cover Designer: Elizabeth Zuhl
Art Producer: Hannah Dickerson
Editor: Brian Sweeting
Production Editor: Sigi Nacson
Production Manager: Holly Haydash

Illustrations © Anugraha Design/Creative Market

Paperback ISBN: 978-1-63807-193-8
R0

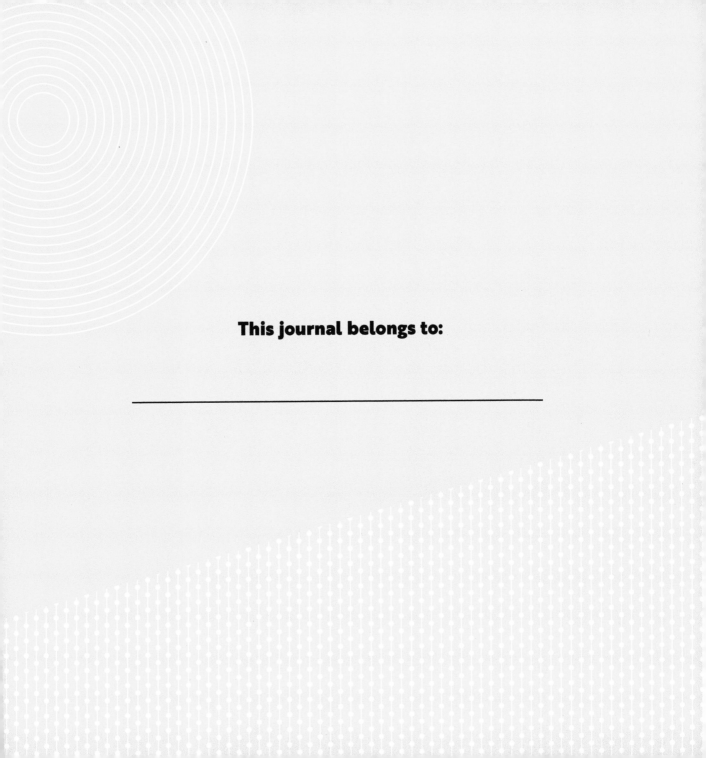

This journal belongs to:

_____

CONTENTS

INTRODUCTION

This journal is a place for you to explore and cope with the changes in your life as your family grows and evolves—we'll call it your blended family. Everyone takes a unique path here. It's likely one or both of your parents have recoupled. Perhaps you have full siblings, stepsiblings, or half-siblings. Although your family might not be how you thought it would be, this is the family you have. You may simply want a place to get your feelings out, or maybe you're realizing the need for more support. However this journal came into your hands, I'm glad you're here.

Use these pages to reflect, release, and understand your emotions. You'll be able to find a way that works for you to relate to this new vision of your family. If it's been a tough road here, you can learn to tolerate and even like your family. Use this journal to deepen those relationships and let them flourish. The purpose of this journal is not just to support you in this time—it's also to help you love the most important thing: *you*. Come along on a journey with me.

My Story

I was in similar shoes when I was your age. My parents divorced when I was six. Recouplings, remarriages, and stepsiblings and half-siblings entered the picture as I grew up. Admittedly, I didn't always make it easy for my parents and stepparents—and that was mostly because I was a hurting teen trying to figure out my place in all of it. I was afraid that my family situation somehow impacted my worth and lovability. It would have been nice if I'd had something to support me in moving through the sometimes confusing and difficult landscape. I was lucky—my parents blended with grace. For a lot of teens, though, that's not the case, and the stress level is high.

I wish I'd known back then that soon it would feel easier. I would grow up and learn to love my hodgepodge of a family. I wish I'd understood how hard it was on the adults in my life, too, which I realized when I became a stepmom myself. Since then, I've become a Licensed Professional Counselor who works with teens and families. I learned how to relate with emotions, how to accept my family and childhood, and how to find joy in life—big, messy family included. I hope my experience serves you as you search for your own joy.

How to Use This Journal

This journal is broken down into sections. Each section includes writing prompts, exercises to practice, quotes to get you reflecting, and affirmations to use when you need a boost. You may find that some of the quotes, practices, or prompts ring truer for you than others. Use what feels right and leave the rest. Perhaps one of them will pack more of a punch later on, or maybe it's just not for you. My hope is you'll find at least one or two moments in this process that give you a sigh of relief. That's where healing starts.

Please be gentle with yourself. If you want to work through each section in order, do so. If you'd rather begin in the back or skip around based on your current needs, do that. Throughout this journal, try your best to stay focused on what is yours—your emotions, your physical sensations, and the quality of your thoughts. This journal is for *you*. Use your experience to help you sort through the feelings, uncertainties, and difficult moments that come up. This journal, however, is simply a guide. You are the master of your own path. Trust yourself, and use these pages in whatever way feels right for you.

Just the Beginning

As a counselor, I must remind you that journaling is simply a stepping-stone. Ideally, you'd share some of what you discover throughout this process with a trusted adult, such as a counselor, an aunt/uncle, a grandparent, a stepparent, or a parent. If you're feeling overtaken by anxiety, sadness, or another difficult emotion, there's no shame in reaching out for help. Ask a parent to assist you in finding the right counselor. If doing so doesn't feel safe, many states allow teens to access counseling on their own.

This process takes time. In the brain, for a skill to progress from an understanding, to a regular practice, to an intentional response, to a natural way of being takes about two years. *Two years!* That's a long time, but it doesn't mean you can't feel immediate improvement. Some of the skills in this journal can bring instant benefit, and identifying and expressing emotion, even once, helps the brain process your feelings more effectively the next time.

You've Got This

Family can be complicated and messy, but also beautiful. We don't get to choose our families, stepparents, or siblings. And you can be intentional about how you learn to relate to yourself and to them to find joy in how your family has evolved. It's possible to effect change, even as a teen. Although it's not your responsibility to create peace in your family, you are more capable than you know. I hope that throughout this process, you'll find your power, respect it, and continue on your journey of loving yourself and your family, however it looks today.

There is no agony like bearing an untold story inside of you.

—ZORA NEALE HURSTON

Start Where You Are

Let's be real—being a teen is hard. You're no longer a kid, but also not quite an adult. You're dealing with the demands of school, the pressure to decide what to do with the rest of your life, and the challenge of balancing the influences of family and friends. Adding a blended family on top of all that can feel over-whelming, especially if you've recently lost your family's original setup. It can be a lot to process, and it will take time. It's hard to believe, but one day, the way your family is now will likely feel normal.

This section will help you get a clearer picture of where you are so you'll have a better vision of where you're going. We'll focus on how your family has changed, what you need, and ways you can care for yourself, inside and out.

The Photo Album of Your Life

Look back through your memory of your life. Is it smooth, like the flow of a river, or does it feel spotty, like pieces are missing? Both are normal. Before reflecting on the prompts in this section, go through your photos and find one picture of your life from each year you've been alive, as best as you can. What do you notice? How does the kid in those pictures feel? What do you wish they knew?

_____

_____

_____

_____

_____

_____

_____

_____

_____

_____

_____

Do you remember your parents being together? If so, what was that like? If not, how does that feel for you? Regardless of whether you remember them together, what is one way you've been impacted by them not being together?

_____

_____

_____

_____

_____

_____

_____

_____

_____

_____

_____

_____

If you remember it, how was your parents' separation? How did they tell you they were separating? What were you thinking or feeling at the time? How did you respond? If you don't remember, how has life been for you since they separated?

_____

_____

_____

_____

_____

_____

_____

_____

_____

_____

_____

_____

_____

_____

_____

How long was it before your new family members came into your life? How were you told about them?

_____

_____

_____

_____

_____

_____

_____

_____

_____

_____

_____

_____

_____

How did you feel about your parent finding another partner? Some kids feel pleased for their parent, wanting them to be happy. Other kids are fearful that they'll lose some attention or love. Still other kids feel loyalty to their other parent, and they struggle to let a new person in. What did it look like for you? How did you share your feelings with your parents?

_____

_____

_____

_____

_____

_____

_____

_____

_____

_____

_____

_____

_____

_____

_____

How has blending been going for you?

_____

_____

_____

_____

_____

_____

_____

_____

_____

_____

_____

_____

_____

_____

Your Emotional Backpack

When we embark on a journey, we usually need to bring a few tools to make the process easier and more enjoyable. Think about what you might pack in your emotional backpack for this blended family trip. Maybe you'll want to bring old memories from your childhood (cartoons on Saturday mornings with your parent), an openness to new relationships (there's always room for more), or some alone time to recharge (sitting outside on a nice day and journaling). List five emotional tools that will help you as you work through this journal.

1. _____

2. _____

3. _____

4. _____

5. _____

When you were younger, what did you imagine your family would be like at your current age? How is life today similar to or different from what you envisioned?

_____

_____

_____

_____

_____

_____

_____

_____

_____

_____

_____

_____

_____

What three moments or events in your life seemed to be key in the development of you? These moments could be big, like when your parents separated, or when you discovered something you love. Or they could be little, like words someone once shared with you. What was so important about these moments, and how does it feel to reflect on them now?

1. _____

_____

_____

_____

_____

2. _____

_____

_____

_____

_____

3. _____

_____

_____

_____

_____

Do you have new stepsiblings or, perhaps, half-siblings? If so, what has it been like for you? What is your relationship like with them?

_____

_____

_____

_____

_____

_____

_____

_____

_____

_____

_____

_____

_____

_____

What about your blended family stresses you most?

_____

_____

_____

_____

_____

_____

_____

_____

_____

_____

_____

_____

_____

_____

What are you most excited or relieved about in terms of your blended family?

_____

_____

_____

_____

_____

_____

_____

_____

_____

_____

_____

_____

Listen to Your Body

Our bodies are a great source of information. Spend a moment listening to your body. Start by taking a few deep breaths. Notice the weight of your body in your seat, and settle into your body. Think about how your family has changed, and jot down some physical sensations you notice in your body in response. Is it tight, heavy, open, hot, knotted, or tingling? Does it change as you breathe? Does it have firm edges, or does it fade outward? Does it have a color or shape?

_____

_____

_____

_____

_____

_____

_____

_____

_____

_____

_____

_____

What are those sensations trying to say? What might they be trying to teach or show you?

_____

_____

_____

_____

_____

_____

_____

_____

_____

_____

_____

_____

_____

What Is True for You?

For these five questions, complete the sentence with what feels true for you:

1. In this new family, I'm afraid . . .

_____

2. Family is supposed to be . . .

_____

3. I'm really looking forward to . . .

_____

4. My family is different now because . . .

_____

5. I'm grateful for . . .

_____

How did that exercise feel for you? What did you notice come up or change in your body?

_____

_____

_____

_____

You don't wake up at 18 and necessarily become the person you want to be as an adult—you have to work hard to become them.

—RUBY ROSE

If you could wake up in six months and have a happy family—keeping in mind that you can't change who is in your family—what would look different from this morning? What can you do to contribute toward that happy family today?

_____

_____

_____

_____

_____

_____

_____

_____

_____

_____

_____

_____

_____

_____

_____

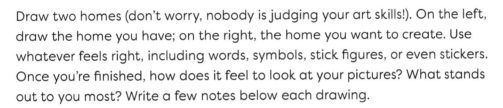

Draw Your Home

Draw two homes (don't worry, nobody is judging your art skills!). On the left, draw the home you have; on the right, the home you want to create. Use whatever feels right, including words, symbols, stick figures, or even stickers. Once you're finished, how does it feel to look at your pictures? What stands out to you most? Write a few notes below each drawing.

A Song for This Moment

Go through your music and find one song that feels like it speaks to you right now. What song is it? What about that song do you like? What lyrics resonate with you most? Return to this song whenever you need to feel understood.

_____

_____

_____

_____

_____

_____

_____

_____

_____

_____

_____

_____

_____

_____

_____

_____

What is a favorite memory you have with your family from when you were little? How might you be able to bring the joy from that day into an experience with your family today? (For example, maybe your family always made heart-shaped pizzas on Valentine's Day. Maybe you could teach your new bonus parent or siblings how it's done.)

Practicing Self-Care Routines

Practicing self-care is essential throughout this process. When a stressor (something that causes stress) presents itself, we respond with feelings of stress. Even after the stressor resolves, we can be left with the stress. Your body needs you to find ways to release that stress each day. The following list includes activities that support you in releasing stress. Pick up to five you'd like to try, and commit to one for the next week:

- Go for a walk.

- Take a shower or bubble bath and focus on your five senses.

- Turn on a song, and sing along as loudly as you can.

- Color in an adult coloring book.

- Go to a private place and scream from your gut.

- Ask a close friend if you can share your *feelings*.

- Do progressive muscle relaxation (see page 41).

- Paint a picture with washable paint, using only your fingers.

- Journal all your feelings, as much as you can, in three minutes.

- Ask someone for a 20-second hug (relax against them).

- Wrap yourself in a soft blanket, then sip your favorite tea.

- Pet or play with an animal.

- Watch your favorite comedy (one that really gets you laughing).

- Count your breath: On each inhale, count 1; on each exhale, count 2.

- Get a good, ugly cry out.

- Meditate (see the Resources section for meditation apps at the end of this journal).

I CARRY MY JOY

WITH ME

WHEREVER I GO.

Tears are words that

need to be shed.

—PAULO COELHO

Feel Your Feelings

Most of us are not taught how to notice, manage, or communicate our emotions. We struggle to connect with them, and we spend a lot of time trying to swallow them, numb them out, or distract ourselves—and social media makes it all too easy.

Emotions are just energy. They're not dangerous, and although they may cause some discomfort, they can't harm you. They can't swallow you whole, and as hard as it may be to believe, you are not your feelings. They are like clouds passing by in the sky. You are not the clouds; you are the sky.

In this section, we'll go through some prompts to help you explore how to relate differently with your emotions. These questions are geared toward helping you not only see the connection between thoughts and feelings, but also learn how to release, express, and feel.

Listening to Your "Belly Brain"

We started learning about emotions in the body in section 1. We'll dig deeper into that now. Juliane Taylor Shore, PhD, talks about having a "belly brain." Just like in your brain, neurons are wrapped around your gut. These neurons send information up to your brain, where it checks four times per second whether you are safe. Wow, right? It is why listening to your body is the biggest skill you can master when it comes to feelings. I'll ask a question, and you'll practice listening to your gut for an answer. The answer may come as images, words, stories, music, or physical sensations (such as tingling, warmth, etc.). Trust your first response, sit with it for a moment, and write it down. How are you really feeling about your new family?

_____

_____

_____

_____

_____

_____

_____

_____

_____

_____

Which part of your family changing has had the biggest impact on you? Why do you think that is?

_____

_____

_____

_____

_____

_____

_____

_____

_____

_____

_____

_____

_____

_____

Name three emotions you're holding on to when it comes to your blended family. Where do these emotions live in your body?

1. _____

_____

_____

_____

_____

_____

2. _____

_____

_____

_____

_____

_____

3. _____

_____

_____

_____

_____

When have you acted as a result of those emotions, and how did it feel to do so?

_____

_____

_____

_____

_____

_____

_____

_____

_____

_____

_____

_____

_____

How You Learned About Emotions

Sit with each of the following questions to help you explore how you learned about emotions. Try to expand beyond just a word or two. Follow up any answer with questions: "Why?" "How does this feel?" "How do I wish it were?"

When someone in my family is angry, they . . .

_____

_____

When I feel sad, I know my family will . . .

_____

_____

My family deals with emotions by . . .

_____

_____

I wish my parents knew I felt . . .

_____

_____

For me, emotions are [scary, useful, annoying] . . .

_____

_____

Disliking feelings is not automatic—we learn it when we're little. Feelings are just energy; they're neutral. We label some as "good" and others as "bad," but in reality, they're just an energy discharge. In fact, you can even learn to *enjoy* your feelings—yes, even the ones we label as bad. Can you think of a time when a "bad" feeling ended up feeling good? (For instance, maybe you hurt someone's feelings and felt guilty, but you were able to mend the relationship and feel more connected as a result.)

_____

_____

_____

_____

_____

_____

_____

_____

_____

_____

_____

Write down three thoughts you regularly have about your family. Next to each thought, write what emotion comes up, along with what you feel in your body when you have that thought.

1. _____

_____

_____

_____

2. _____

_____

_____

_____

3. _____

_____

_____

_____

What is your favorite emotion to experience? Describe a time when that emotion felt big for you.

_____

_____

_____

_____

_____

_____

_____

_____

_____

_____

_____

_____

_____

_____

_____

Sitting with Emotions

We all want to be able to fully experience our emotions without feeling overwhelmed, and act from our wise self instead of reacting from within big feelings. Here is a practice to strengthen this skill. The process has a few steps I encourage you to try. It may feel difficult at first, but the more you practice, the easier it'll become.

1. Notice the whoosh of emotion as it comes up in your body.

2. Choose to let that emotion stay with you, and sit with it in your body.

3. Breathe, and watch as the emotion moves through you. It could be one breath, or ten minutes of breathing.

See if there's something your body is trying to teach you. This exercise is all about listening to your body, not your mind. You can't think your way out of emotions. When an emotion arises, your thoughts serve only to make the emotion bigger. If you focus on just the physical sensations, your emotions will rise, peak, and crash within a few minutes.

If you get to ten minutes, distract yourself with something comforting. If you're still feeling the depths of an emotion at ten minutes, you're thinking about it without realizing it. When we ride the waves of emotion, we find we can feel them without acting from them.

Is there something you could forgive your family for? What is it, and how would it feel to truly let that go?

_____

_____

_____

_____

_____

_____

_____

_____

_____

_____

_____

_____

_____

What emotion is the hardest for you to sit with? Where does it come from?

_____

_____

_____

_____

_____

_____

_____

_____

_____

_____

_____

_____

_____

_____

_____

_____

What is one hurt you're struggling to let go of?

_____

_____

_____

_____

_____

_____

When you think about that hurt, how do you react? Do you tense up around it, try to push it away, or ache to distract or busy yourself?

_____

_____

_____

_____

_____

_____

_____

➡ See if you can give the hurt permission to be with you in your body. You can set a timer for two minutes and simply breathe with the hurt. It may be uncomfortable, but it can't harm you. You can do just about anything for two minutes. What about that hurt is becoming hard to hold on to?

_____

_____

_____

_____

_____

➡ How would your life change if you were able to let go of that hurt?

_____

_____

_____

_____

_____

_____

_____

Emotions are what make you human, and all the good stuff—joy, love, excitement—comes from there. You can't have those emotions without also experiencing disappointment, fear, and sadness. When you feel like you can't handle the difficult emotions, what might you be able to say to comfort, encourage, or support yourself?

_____

_____

_____

_____

_____

_____

_____

_____

_____

_____

_____

_____

Here's the good news: If you lean into difficult emotions, they move along like waves of the ocean and leave more room for the good stuff afterward. When we hold on to emotions by numbing them, trying to swallow them, or ignoring them, they become more powerful and take up extra room. Name a time when you've really gone through an emotion (like sobbing over the loss of something), and describe how you felt afterward. Was there more space?

_____

_____

_____

_____

_____

_____

_____

_____

_____

_____

_____

_____

Relax Your Muscles

Progressive muscle relaxation is a technique that can relax your nervous system and make the difference between tension and relaxation clearer for you (just like we talked about with releasing stress in section 1).

Sit or lie down somewhere comfortable. You can have gentle music playing, or be in silence. Once you've read the following instructions, close your eyes if you're comfortable doing so.

1. Start by taking a few deep breaths.

2. Imagine breathing in through the top of your head, watching your breath move through your body, and breathing out through your toes.

3. Beginning with your toes, flex and tighten your muscles as hard as you can for three seconds, then fully relax them.

4. Do the same with your feet: Flex for three seconds, then relax.

5. Continue the process, moving up through your body—your shins, calves, knees, thighs, hips, stomach, etc. Flex one muscle at a time for three seconds, then relax.

How do you feel after practicing progressive muscle relaxation? Can you see yourself applying this technique again in a certain situation? What is it?

_____

_____

_____

What Brings You Stress and Comfort?

Create two lists. In one list, write down five things that bring stress or overwhelm you. In the other, write down five things that bring comfort or relax you.

Things that bring stress:

1. _____

2. _____

3. _____

4. _____

5. _____

Things that bring comfort:

1. _____

2. _____

3. _____

4. _____

5. _____

What is one way you could commit to putting down a stress you no longer need to carry, and instead picking up something that comforts you?

_____

_____

_____

_____

_____

_____

_____

_____

_____

_____

_____

_____

_____

_____

Feelings Are Only One Source of Information

Sometimes we use our emotions to guide our reasoning, which means we tell ourselves, "If I feel it, it must be true." Feelings are a source of information for us, but they're only one of our sources. Believing that feelings must be true because we feel them is a thought error—and often a painful way of thinking.

You've probably experienced this when a friend didn't message you back. Did you say something wrong? Are they okay? Anxiety floods your system. Then you hear from them, and they report that they spent the last three hours tearing apart their room to find their phone. Phew. Just because you felt anxiety didn't mean they were upset with you or hurt.

Think of a time you've felt this way: You were sure of something, you had an emotional response, then you found out later that it wasn't true. What was the emotion that came up for you? What did you tell yourself to recover?

_____

What can you use from that experience to help you when your feelings get loud again?

_____

Knowing that "If I feel it, it must be true" is a thought error, what is one emotion you've been holding on to about your family that you've been stuck believing? What could you do to relax your grip on it?

_____

You can learn to sense the good feelings in your body. Think about a time when you were really happy. Maybe you were laughing with a friend, being comforted by someone you love, or feeling truly seen and listened to. Bring back the situation in your mind until you feel it in your body.

Write down the happy memory, along with the physical sensations you notice when you revisit that time.

_____

_____

_____

_____

_____

_____

_____

_____

_____

_____

_____

_____

_____

Let's come up with an emotion regulation mantra. (A mantra is a statement you can tell yourself when you need a boost or a reminder.) Spend a moment reviewing what you've learned about emotions and yourself in this section. What do you want to take with you? (Here are some examples: "I am the sky, not the clouds," "I can ride the wave of this emotion," and "Emotions are just energy.")

_____

_____

_____

_____

_____

_____

_____

_____

_____

_____

_____

_____

When we bring awareness to our emotions, something truly amazing happens. They lose their power to make us miserable.

—DZOGCHEN PONLOP RINPOCHE

Write down ten things that make you smile just thinking about them.

1. _____

_____

_____

2. _____

_____

_____

3. _____

_____

_____

4. _____

_____

_____

5. _____

_____

_____

6. _____

_____

_____

7. _____

_____

_____

8. _____

_____

_____

9. _____

_____

_____

10. _____

_____

_____

How would your life change if you saw your emotions as friends? If you were happy to have emotions come up, how would you relate differently with them or speak differently to yourself?

_____

_____

_____

_____

_____

_____

_____

_____

_____

_____

_____

_____

_____

_____

I RESPECT MY
FEELINGS AND
ACCEPT THEM
AS THEY ARE.

Self-compassion is simply giving the same kindness to ourselves that we would give to others.

—CHRISTOPHER GERMER, PhD

Boost Your Self-Compassion and Self-Love

Becoming part of a blended family brings up a lot of questions for everyone. It's easy to question how you fit in, worry that there's no room for your feelings, or fear that when families grow, the amount of love and time for you will shrink.

Ultimately, your worth is inherent. That means you were born with it—it can't be added to or lost. You earned the right to be here the day you were born. Be gentle with yourself and your feelings. Remind yourself often that you're just trying to figure it out.

This section will explore ways you can tap into loving yourself more freely. Holding yourself with honesty, acknowledging the beautiful and challenging parts of yourself, and choosing to soften toward all the corners of you can create space for real self-love. Model for your family the way you want to be seen and treated—with kindness, understanding, and love.

Write down ten words to describe yourself.

1. _____

2. _____

3. _____

4. _____

5. _____

6. _____

7. _____

8. _____

9. _____

10. _____

What qualities, skills, interests, characteristics, or talents make you unique?

_____

_____

_____

_____

_____

_____

_____

_____

_____

_____

_____

_____

_____

_____

Unconditional love is a warm wish for someone to be happy, regardless of what might move or change within the relationship. How would it feel—or how does it feel—to love yourself unconditionally? How can you show it?

_____

_____

_____

_____

_____

_____

_____

_____

_____

_____

_____

_____

_____

_____

How have the changes in your family impacted how you feel about yourself?

_____

_____

_____

_____

_____

_____

_____

_____

_____

_____

_____

_____

_____

Draw Your Heart Space

Draw a heart (bonus points if it's imperfect!). Inside the heart, draw the different emotions that make up your heart. You can use symbols, colors, or patterns. Then sit with your heart for a moment, noticing how your body feels.

What does looking at your heart teach you?

Do you treat yourself kindly? In what situations does it get difficult for you to do so? Do you sometimes get stuck?

_____

_____

_____

_____

_____

_____

_____

_____

_____

_____

_____

_____

_____

_____

Describe a time when you acted compassionately toward a friend in need. How might you be able to offer yourself the same compassion?

_____

_____

_____

_____

_____

_____

_____

_____

_____

_____

_____

_____

_____

_____

_____

_____

_____

_____

Sending Yourself Compassion

Take a moment to send yourself some compassion:

1. Sit comfortably, and start with a few deep breaths. Notice where you feel breath most in your body. It might be the warm or cool air in your nose or in your throat, or the rise and fall of your chest.

2. If you wish, place a hand or both hands on your heart. Notice the pressure and warmth of your hand(s) on your chest. Or simply notice any sensation in your chest that comes up for you.

3. Pay attention and allow your body to breathe, noticing what comes up. See if you can soften toward yourself, including any emotions or physical tension, and offer those places some kindness.

4. Sit with it as long as it feels comforting.

Write down any thoughts or feelings you have after sending yourself compassion.

_____

_____

_____

_____

_____

_____

How has your relationship with yourself been lately? Do you give yourself the attention, care, and fun you need? What could make this relationship better?

_____

_____

_____

_____

_____

_____

_____

_____

_____

_____

_____

_____

_____

_____

_____

_____

Identifying Real Self-Worth

Terry Real, creator of Relational Life Therapy—a type of relationship counseling that aims to help people be more accountable, authentic, and relational in their approach to one another—describes three types of false self-worth:

1. **Performance-based.** We measure our worth based on how well we perform—but then we're only ever "as good as our last game."

2. **Attribute-based.** Our worth is based on something that we have or are. You have worth because you're pretty, smart, or have a nice phone. But what happens when you lose that someday?

3. **Other-based.** We think, "I don't have self-worth, but I do if *you* think I do." This belief can make us chase relationships and reassurance.

When you're struggling, which type do you identify with most? What is it like to acknowledge that?

_____

Alternatively, real self-worth comes from seeing yourself honestly and still feeling a loving warmth toward yourself. It's just like when you see faults in your friends but you still adore them. There is love despite imperfections. What are three imperfections that you could choose to love about you?

1. _____

2. _____

3. _____

Finish the following sentences. Spend some time thinking about them, and be honest with yourself.

I really wish I could change . . .

_____

_____

I really love that I . . .

_____

_____

The idea of failing makes me feel . . .

_____

_____

I am really good at . . .

_____

_____

I feel pressured to . . .

_____

_____

What fears do you have around how your worth, value, or place in your family will be different as your family changes and grows?

_____

_____

_____

_____

_____

_____

_____

_____

_____

_____

_____

_____

_____

Words That Hurt

Words can't upset us without our permission. If we don't believe what someone says about us, it can't hurt our feelings. If someone calls you a stove, you probably won't feel offended. Why? Because it's ridiculous. You know you're *not* a stove. But if someone calls you something you believe about yourself (such as ugly, dumb, or annoying), suddenly the word stings.

How you talk to yourself and the beliefs you hold about yourself matter. Life is hard enough—we don't need to add to it by bullying ourselves. Write down some negative thoughts you have about yourself and how those views make you feel. Then describe one way you can work on letting go of those beliefs today.

_____

_____

_____

_____

_____

_____

_____

_____

Replacing Negative Self-Talk

One way you can combat negative self-talk is to work on replacing a harsh tone with a kinder, more loving voice. Here's an example of not getting the grade you'd hoped for on a school project.

Instead of: "What is wrong with me?"

Try: "Hey, I hear you're worried and disappointed about how that turned out. Thanks for trying to take care of me."

Then switch to: "I tried really hard on that, and I'm disappointed. It's okay to be disappointed. How about I go on a walk to take care of me?"

Name a time when you spoke negatively toward yourself. Walk through these steps to offer that voice some kindness, then switch it up.

_____

_____

_____

_____

_____

_____

_____

_____

Is there something you need to forgive yourself for? How might you do that?

_____

_____

_____

_____

_____

_____

_____

_____

_____

_____

_____

_____

_____

_____

_____

_____

What is one internal habit that doesn't feel good that you could change with some effort? What about a good habit you could engage in more? (For instance, perhaps you'd like to stop looking on the negative side of things so much, and be more honest about your emotions.)

_____

_____

_____

_____

_____

_____

_____

_____

_____

_____

_____

_____

Where is your favorite place to be at home? Why?

_____

_____

_____

_____

_____

_____

_____

_____

_____

_____

_____

_____

_____

_____

_____

_____

What is one thing that would bring you joy to learn, experience, or practice? What is a step you could take this week toward achieving it?

_____

_____

_____

_____

_____

_____

_____

_____

_____

_____

_____

_____

_____

_____

What are three things that help you feel safe and soothed? Can you access them easily, or would you benefit from finding a few more supportive things, people, or places?

1. _____

_____

_____

_____

2. _____

_____

_____

_____

3. _____

_____

_____

_____

What do you need to do to be more at peace with yourself? Maybe you have some unhelpful beliefs you could let go of, or you could take more time to care for yourself or engage in a passion.

What are you most grateful for in your life? When you think of these things, can you feel your body opening up? How might this feeling be helpful during tough times?

_____

_____

_____

_____

_____

_____

_____

_____

_____

_____

_____

_____

_____

Draw the Superhero Version of You

Get some drawing materials—pencils, markers, crayons, or paint—and draw yourself as a superhero. What is your special power? What is your weakness? How are you a force for good? You can step into your superhero self whenever you need to. Stand up tall, look up and slightly to the side, and put your hands on your hips. With your chest open and toward the sky, take in three deep breaths. This practice tricks your brain into feeling more powerful. (Or maybe it just lets your real power shine through.)

Start a New Practice

Pick one of these activities to practice this week as a way of intentionally caring for yourself:

- Choose one afternoon to disconnect from screens (phone, tablet, computer, TV). Take time to relax and unwind without the worry of notifications.

- Write a love letter to yourself. Seal it, and mark a date in your calendar to open it in a few months when you need a boost.

- Write down a decision you made during the week that you're proud of.

- Make a fun plan with family or friends in the next week that you'll look forward to.

- Stretch for five minutes before bed three times this week.

So why is self-compassion a more effective motivator than self-criticism? Because its driving force is love, not fear.

—KRISTIN NEFF, PhD

➤ Write down the words you need to hear—words of encouragement, empathy, or hope.

_____

_____

_____

_____

_____

_____

_____

_____

_____

_____

_____

_____

_____

_____

_____

I CHOOSE TO BE
KIND TO MYSELF
IN THIS MOMENT.

It's the attitude about life, man. Looking at the light instead of the dark. Looking at love instead of fear.

—QUINCY JONES

Navigate New Relationships

Families grow and change—especially in blended families, where you suddenly have a bunch of new relationships. You know you don't get to choose family, but you're used to them because you never knew life without them. Now you have *new* family you're not used to—and you didn't choose them, either.

Relationships in blended families aren't meant to replace anyone. Think of them as bonus relationships. You may experience weird moments as your old relationships shift, confusion around where your loyalty should be, and uncertainty about what these new family members expect.

This section is all about learning how to live with these new folks in your life without losing sight of yourself. It's possible to have healthy boundaries, build trust, and create lasting connections with your new family members. Relaxing into these relationships can help release some of the difficult emotions and tensions that come with a blended family.

Your Growing Family

Take a moment to consider all the new relationships that have come into your life. It's never just a parent's new partner—they come with their own friends and family who are woven into your life as well. Make a list of all the relationships you've gained (think new partner, grandparents, aunts, uncles, siblings, friends, etc.). How does it feel to see on paper just how big your family has grown?

_____

_____

_____

_____

_____

_____

_____

_____

_____

_____

_____

_____

_____

_____

How does it feel to think of your parent's new partner and their people as family? Does it change how you feel or think about the word "family"?

_____

_____

_____

_____

_____

_____

_____

_____

_____

_____

_____

_____

_____

_____

How You Feel About Family

Complete the following sentences.

Three things I like about my new family are . . .

_____

_____

_____

My new family might be able to teach me . . .

_____

_____

Three things I'm not sure I like about my new family yet are . . .

_____

_____

_____

The good that will come from my new family is . . .

_____

I'm most nervous about . . .

_____

Sitting with New Experiences

Spend some time thinking about something you've done that was new and difficult (for example, entering high school, trying out for a team, making a new friend). Notice the feelings that came up for you—the thoughts, doubts, and nerves that may have been there. Feel through each experience in your body, and offer them a little compassion. *Of course that was difficult.* Now that you're past the experience, how did you grow from it? How might you grow from this experience of having a blended family?

_____

_____

_____

_____

_____

_____

_____

_____

_____

_____

_____

Whenever we add new people into our family, all the original relationships have to move and shift to create space. If you have younger siblings, you've likely experienced it. One key to making the shifting around successful is paying attention to your outlook. What are some expectations you have about how this blended family should be?

_____

_____

_____

_____

_____

_____

_____

_____

_____

_____

_____

_____

_____

_____

_____

_____

How does it feel to reflect on the hopes you have for your family? What do you think those expectations are trying to protect you from or teach you? How might they be holding you back?

_____

_____

_____

_____

_____

_____

_____

_____

_____

_____

_____

_____

_____

_____

Struggle comes from the difference between what you expect and your reality. Try to let go of any awkwardness from past interactions, knowing that everyone is doing the best they can. Sticking with expectations only holds back the potential for connection. What might it be like if you met each day with your family as new instead of firmly holding on to a set of expectations? If you felt curious about your family in each interaction, how might your relationships change?

_____

_____

_____

_____

_____

_____

_____

_____

_____

_____

_____

_____

Feel It in Your Body

Spend a few minutes settling into your body. Focus on your breath, and feel where your body makes contact with your seat. From this settled place, ask yourself, "What does family mean to me?" Write down your answer.

_____

_____

_____

_____

_____

After expressing what family means to you, how do you feel? What comes up in your body? Do you find any tension in your body around that belief?

_____

_____

_____

_____

_____

_____

Have you received any messages from your other parent about how to feel about this new part of your family? (For example, some parents will encourage you to be open to your new family, some will remain stony silent, and others may have an opinion about new family members.)

_____

_____

_____

_____

_____

_____

_____

_____

_____

_____

_____

_____

_____

_____

_____

What do you think about the messages you've received from the other parent about how to feel? Do these messages impact how you relate to your blended family?

_____

_____

_____

_____

_____

_____

_____

_____

_____

_____

_____

_____

_____

_____

_____

What worries are you holding on to when it comes to this new family and your other parent? (Some teens are concerned about loyalty, for instance. Others worry their parents will struggle with healthy boundaries—for example, they'll fight with each other through their kids, or they'll ask their kids too many prying questions about the other family to get information.) Is it okay to like a new family member?

_____

_____

_____

_____

_____

_____

_____

_____

_____

_____

_____

_____

Strong communities are born out of individuals being their best selves.

—LEANNE BETASAMOSAKE SIMPSON

Before and After

Draw a picture of yourself (stick figures allowed!). Then, using a specific color for each of the two questions that follow, make notes and label the thoughts, physical sensations, and emotions that show up throughout your body.

First color: What did you feel when you first met the new members of your family? (Examples are nervous tension in your shoulders, excited butterflies in your stomach, hopefulness about the relationship, or distress as a result of the changes.)

Second color: How are you feeling about your new family members today? (Examples are less tension, more openness, increased uncertainty, or struggling with feeling accepted.)

How might you relax into your new family? What are two ways you could let that openness influence the way you interact with your blended family this week?

1. _____

_____

_____

_____

_____

_____

_____

2. _____

_____

_____

_____

_____

_____

_____

What support do you need from your parents to settle in with your blended family? (For example, do you need some alone time or would you like to carve out special time with certain family members?)

_____

_____

_____

_____

_____

_____

_____

_____

_____

_____

_____

_____

_____

_____

_____

Holding Both

Some of the most meaningful things in life come with the most difficulty. To have wonderful experiences, we have to accept the challenging times, too.

1. Find an index card and a pen. On one side of the index card, write "Meaningful," and on the other, write "Difficult."

2. On the meaningful side, write down things about family that matter to you. (It could sound like belonging, kindness, connection, and/or fun.) Who do you want family to be? How do you hope to feel? How do you plan to act from within your idea of what family means?

3. On the back of the index card, write down the difficult thoughts or emotions that might show up when you try to put into action what matters to you.

4. Keep this card with you in a notebook, wallet, or backpack. When things get hard, remind yourself that you can't have anything meaningful without difficulty—all things in life come with both. The difficulty doesn't take away the joy of experiencing what is meaningful.

Look through your music and find a song that speaks to you about overcoming a difficult experience. What song is it? Write down some of the lyrics that ring true for you. How do you feel listening to those lyrics?

_____

_____

_____

_____

_____

_____

_____

_____

_____

_____

_____

_____

_____

_____

_____

_____

What Are Your Responsibilities in Your Family?

Write down five things you believe are your responsibility in your blended family. These could be messages you've received or beliefs you have.

It is my responsibility to . . .

Example: It is my responsibility to be kind with my words.

1. _____

2. _____

3. _____

4. _____

5. _____

Reflect on your list of responsibilities. Are there any that aren't really yours to keep? If you're feeling accountable for something that really should be a parent's concern—like creating an atmosphere of peace in the family—can you replace it with a responsibility that is, in fact, yours?

_____

_____

All healthy relationships have boundaries, which we'll talk more about in section 5. For now, what is one boundary you need? It could be emotional (having space when you need to process), physical (someone knocking before they enter your room), or mental (not taking everything someone says personally).

_____

_____

_____

_____

_____

_____

_____

_____

_____

_____

_____

_____

_____

_____

_____

Trust takes time. It is built slowly over repeated incidents. These experiences give us confidence that we can count on others, and they let others know they can rely on us.

What is one positive thing you can count on from your family?

_____

_____

_____

_____

What is one thing your family can rely on from you?

_____

_____

_____

_____

What can you do this week to build and care for the trust in your relationships?

_____

_____

_____

_____

Family Circle

Create a collage of what your idea of family looks like. You can be as resourceful as you like: Draw or doodle using markers, pencils, or crayons; ask a parent for old magazines and cut out images you're drawn to; or print out photos you find online.

As you're making your collage, think about how your family has been, what it has become, and how you'd like to see it in the future, as well as how it feels for you.

You've finished your collage. How does it feel to look at it? What do you notice about how your family circle looks?

Everyone has good parts, difficult parts, and unpleasant parts. What we focus on becomes what feels true for us. What is something interesting, fun, or silly you've learned about each of your new family members? How might focusing on those brighter parts ease your relationships?

_____

_____

_____

_____

_____

_____

_____

_____

_____

_____

_____

_____

_____

_____

_____

_____

What is the biggest issue getting in the way of you enjoying your new family? (For example, maybe you don't feel invited into the relationship, you're feeling stubborn, or you struggle with knowing how to connect.) What is one thing you can do to make it easier?

_____

_____

_____

_____

_____

_____

_____

_____

_____

_____

_____

_____

_____

_____

_____

Gratitude can relax even the toughest of moods. Write down three things you're genuinely grateful for in your family and life. They could be simple, like having a comfortable home or feeling safe. Or they could be more specific, like having an animal or a great stepparent. On a tough day, return to what fills your body with gratitude.

1. _____

_____

_____

_____

2. _____

_____

_____

_____

3. _____

_____

_____

_____

I KNOW THAT EVERYONE IS DOING THE BEST THEY CAN AT EVERY MOMENT, INCLUDING ME.

To know how much there is to know is the beginning of learning to live.

—DOROTHY WEST

Communicate Your Needs

Communication is the glue that holds relationships together. And communication for teens can be hard. Parents and teens often get into a difficult cycle: Parents assume teens are being unnecessarily emotional, and teens assume parents don't care or don't understand. In these moments, nobody feels good about the relationship—but the cycle can't continue if just one person steps out of it.

In this section, we'll practice ways you can understand your needs, express them in a healthy way, and navigate weird moments or disagreements with grace. It won't go smoothly all the time, but you might just surprise your parents—and yourself—by how well you can learn to communicate what you need.

It will take courage, especially if things with your family are tense right now. As you learn how to identify and communicate your needs, you'll feel more comfortable in your own skin—and it will help your relationships heal and grow.

Identifying Your Wants and Needs

Let's have a look at the differences between wants and needs. A want is something that would be nice to have—for instance, being able to listen to music while doing homework if that's your preference, or having ketchup with your grilled cheese. It's different from a need, which is something you require for survival. Needs are universal. Examples are being seen, being safe, and having a sense of belonging.

Write down five things that you might wish for as your family is changing, then think about whether they are needs or wants. Be honest with yourself. Notice how sometimes a want *feels* like a need (that doesn't mean it is!).

1. _____

2. _____

3. _____

4. _____

5. _____

When you notice that a need is unmet in your life, what does it feel like in your body? What thoughts come up when that need is not being met?

_____

_____

_____

_____

_____

_____

_____

_____

_____

_____

_____

_____

_____

_____

Describe a time when you needed something, and someone was able to meet that need. Maybe you needed someone to listen, and a friend came through. Maybe you needed help with something, and a family member or teacher showed up. What does it feel like to have a need met?

_____

_____

_____

_____

_____

_____

_____

_____

_____

_____

_____

_____

_____

Name one preference that often feels like a need for you. What could you do over the next week to let go of that preference a little? How much stress could letting go of it relieve for you?

_____

_____

_____

_____

_____

_____

_____

_____

_____

_____

_____

_____

_____

_____

_____

▶ What is one way you can keep your focus on your needs as you interact with your family?

_____

_____

_____

_____

_____

_____

▶ What needs of their own might your family members be communicating with you?

_____

_____

_____

_____

_____

_____

➤ If my family really knew me, they would know (list three things) . . .

Example: If my family really knew me, they would know I really do care.

1. _____

_____

_____

2. _____

_____

_____

3. _____

_____

_____

Boundary Bubble

Sit for a moment and imagine feeling safe, peaceful, confident, and comforted. When you're in this place, what image comes to mind? You might imagine yourself surrounded by water, a bubble, or a color, for example Within your image, know you're safe and you can do this. Let the image comfort you. Allow in from others only what is useful to you, and let others have their own perspectives. Remember you can return to this image whenever you need support in a relationship, such as when you're feeling disconnected or after a disagreement.

If you feel frustrated with, overwhelmed by, or withdrawn from a situation or relationship, you probably have an unmet need, and you must set a boundary.

Think of a time when you've felt frustrated, overwhelmed, or withdrawn. What boundary might that emotion have been asking you to set? (For example, maybe you needed to advocate for your or someone else's emotional or physical safety, or perhaps you needed to feel heard, respected, or included.)

_____

_____

_____

_____

_____

_____

_____

_____

_____

_____

_____

_____

_____

Check Your Intentions

Our intentions count for a lot. If we wash the dishes that someone else leaves in the sink, are we doing it to make them feel guilty, to get them to give us something we want, or because we simply want to contribute to our family? Intention sets us up for how we feel in our relationships.

Bring to mind a time when you did (or didn't do) something, and your intentions weren't the best. Put yourself back in that moment in your mind, noticing the thoughts, feelings, urges, and physical sensations that come up. Describe the experience. How do you feel now about the choice (to do or not to do something) you made then? If you could go back and change something, would you? If so, what?

_____

_____

_____

_____

_____

_____

_____

_____

_____

Weird moments happen in relationships, and those moments can make us want to step back. We all get awkward sometimes, and getting to know someone is riddled with potentially awkward moments. Name a weird or awkward moment you could use forgiveness for, and one you could forgive a new family member for.

_____

_____

_____

_____

_____

_____

_____

_____

_____

_____

_____

_____

_____

How do you feel about conflict? Think of a disagreement you've had with a friend. How well do you feel you managed it? If you could improve one way that you manage conflict, what would it be? How might you accomplish it?

_____

_____

_____

_____

_____

_____

_____

_____

_____

_____

_____

_____

_____

Conflict Perspective

Think of a conflict that feels like it comes up a lot in your family. Create a representation of what that conflict looks like. You can use symbols or words, or you can draw the scene. After you've finished, sit with your creation for a moment. What does it feel like to look at it from the outside?

Listening and trying to understand the needs of those we would communicate with seems to me to be the essential prerequisite of any real communication. And we might as well aim for real communication.

—FRED ROGERS

Forgiveness is a vital part of relationships. Sometimes the people in your life, even with the best of intentions, will miss meeting your needs—just like sometimes you'll miss theirs. Forgiveness reminds us we're all human, and we all make mistakes. It brings up the compassion we talked about in section 3.

Name a conflict, a weird moment, or a choice to act with not-so-great intentions. Who needs forgiveness in that situation? If it's you, can you forgive yourself? If it's someone else, can you forgive them? What happens when both people need forgiveness?

Can you think of a time you felt really listened to and understood by someone? How did you know? What did it feel like in your body? How did it change the relationship?

_____

_____

_____

_____

_____

_____

_____

_____

_____

_____

_____

_____

_____

_____

_____

_____

Use Your I-Statements

"I-statements" help us focus on what we're feeling when we communicate with others, as opposed to focusing on trying to control or change others' opinions. Here are two examples.

Instead of: "Why do you always blame me for things?"

Try: "I feel like I sometimes get blamed for things I don't do, and that really hurts my feelings."

Instead of: "Today was supposed to be just us!"

Try: "I'm feeling disappointed. I was really looking forward to time as just us."

Can you feel the difference between the two approaches? We want to communicate our emotions instead of communicating *from* our emotions. Write about three times that you communicated from your emotions. Then write three I-statements that would have better communicated how you were feeling.

Things I communicated
from emotions:

1. _____

2. _____

3. _____

Rewritten as
I-statements:

1. _____

2. _____

3. _____

How do you feel about compromise? In what situations is it easier or harder to compromise?

_____

_____

_____

_____

_____

_____

_____

_____

_____

_____

_____

_____

_____

_____

_____

In relationships, we want to hold ourselves and others as having equal importance. One way we can show it is in managing disagreements.

If you disagree with someone, you can look for the needs that each person is communicating and ask: What solution would meet both people's needs? For example, your parent wants you home early, and you want to stay out late. They want to give you boundaries and keep you safe, and you want to practice independence. Together you can look for solutions that help keep you safe while giving you some independence.

Describe a disagreement you've had with your family about blending. What was the need that each person was trying to communicate? Can you think of a solution that would meet everyone's needs?

_____

_____

_____

_____

_____

_____

_____

_____

_____

What barriers are keeping you from communicating your needs? (Examples of barriers are feeling like what we have to say doesn't matter, not spending enough time understanding our own needs, or getting overwhelmed quickly in disagreements.)

_____

_____

_____

_____

_____

_____

_____

_____

_____

_____

_____

_____

_____

_____

What skill have you learned so far through using this journal that could help you remove or reduce that barrier?

_____

_____

_____

_____

_____

_____

_____

_____

_____

_____

_____

_____

_____

_____

Know Your Values

Note: This exercise has been adapted from "Personal Values Card Sort," MotivationalInterviewing.org.

Being aware of our values helps us to live in a more authentic, connected way. Look through this list, and mark your top five values.

- ⬜ To be accepted as I am
- ⬜ To be independent
- ⬜ To have a comfortable life
- ⬜ To feel concern for others
- ⬜ To be creative
- ⬜ To be dependable
- ⬜ To have a happy family

- ⬜ To keep growing
- ⬜ To be honest
- ⬜ To have valuable knowledge
- ⬜ To love and be loved
- ⬜ To be open to new experiences
- ⬜ To have space for myself

Out of those you selected, can you pick your top three? How does it feel to let two go?

_____

In what ways are you living and acting within your values right now?

_____

In what ways are you living or acting outside your values?

_____

If you could tell someone new in your family one honest and kind truth, what would it be?

_____

_____

_____

_____

_____

_____

_____

_____

_____

_____

_____

_____

_____

You deserve to recognize and communicate your needs and to have your needs met, just like everyone else. Communicating can make you vulnerable, but vulnerability is a strength. It takes courage to show up. Write something that helps you remember you're worth it. It could be something you've learned in this journal, something a friend has told you, or a comforting memory.

I CAN SPEAK MY
TRUTH: HONESTLY
AND WITH LOVE.

The richness, beauty, and depths of love can only be fully experienced in a climate of complete openness, honesty, and vulnerability.

—ANTHONY VENN-BROWN

Take Small Steps Forward

Adjusting to a new family takes time. Your original family wasn't made overnight, either. Exploring all the topics in this journal—emotions, self-compassion, relationships, and communication—might have changed the way you experience your family. It's okay if it hasn't. Either way, see if you can let go of any pressure for it to be a certain way.

Try to take it one day at a time. It won't be perfect—no family is. When times get difficult, return to the skills and lessons you've learned about yourself throughout this journal. You can get through it. You are not responsible for how your family functions moving forward, but you are responsible for how you respond to how your family changes. Ask for help when you need it, be gentle with yourself, and stick to what's true for you.

How has your definition or experience of family changed since you started this journal?

_____

_____

_____

_____

_____

_____

_____

_____

_____

_____

_____

_____

_____

_____

Name one small step you have learned from this journal that you can take right away. Perhaps it's speaking up about a preference you have, or catching negative self-talk and offering that part of you a little kindness.

_____

_____

_____

_____

_____

_____

_____

_____

_____

_____

_____

_____

_____

_____

Have Patience

What is patience, exactly? It's the ability to remain calm and keep your peace even when faced with a difficult or irritating person, situation, or thing (your favorite box of cereal is mysteriously empty on a morning you were looking forward to it, for example). Everyone has some capacity for patience, and we can also grow our capacity for patience by looking for opportunities.

Think of a situation when you're regularly irritated, annoyed, or itchy about having to wait. Maybe you're waiting for something to happen in school, or for a family member to get ready, or for an order to arrive. Put yourself fully in that moment in your mind. Walk through the situation, and notice where impatience comes up in your body—then pause. Instead of acting out in your mind, sink into impatience. What does it feel like in your body? How does it move and change? Does it have a color? What happens if you breathe into it? What happens if you offer it a few kind words?

What is one part of your blended family that you're struggling to have patience with? What would it be like to stay peaceful and calm inside? How might that change your experience?

_____

_____

_____

_____

_____

_____

_____

_____

_____

_____

_____

_____

_____

Name one thing you'd appreciate your family having more patience with you about. What would it feel like to be met with patience for that? How might you offer yourself a little more patience?

_____

_____

_____

_____

_____

_____

_____

_____

_____

_____

_____

_____

_____

You're not obligated to win.
You're obligated to keep
trying to do the best
you can every day.

—MARIAN WRIGHT EDELMAN

Find Your Happy Place

Think of something in your life that brings you incredible joy. Perhaps you're cuddling with a pet, on a beach, at your favorite park, or laughing with someone you love. As you go deeper into the thought, close your eyes. Sink into the full experience, scanning each of your five senses in that moment. What does it feel, look, smell, and sound like? Is there a taste? Breathe into it, and let it wash through your body until you feel yourself relax and open. Stay here as long as you need to, and return any time you need comfort.

Comfort is an important resource. What brings you comfort? It could be an object, a reminder of your strength, or a piece of chocolate. What about something that brings you comfort with your family? Maybe you have Sunday morning smoothies, a special way of saying good-bye, or another comforting ritual.

_____

_____

_____

_____

_____

_____

_____

_____

_____

_____

_____

_____

List three small steps that you can take to be more comfortable, connected, and relaxed with your family.

Example: I can ask my family members how their day was each day, and truly care about their responses.

1. _____
_____
_____
_____

2. _____
_____
_____
_____

3. _____
_____
_____
_____

Who, outside your family, can you rely on for emotional support when you need it? How have they supported you in the past?

_____

_____

_____

_____

_____

_____

_____

_____

_____

_____

_____

_____

Everyone struggles with asking for help at times. Being human, though, means that we need others. Think of a time you needed help but didn't want to ask for it. Maybe you didn't understand a homework assignment, or you got into a weird situation with a friend. How did it feel not to ask for help? Looking back on it, what help could you have asked for?

_____

_____

_____

_____

_____

_____

_____

_____

_____

_____

_____

_____

_____

_____

_____

_____

Name something you could use support with right now. Then think of someone you could ask for help. How might you ask for that help? What could you ask for that would feel supportive?

_____

_____

_____

_____

_____

_____

_____

_____

_____

_____

_____

_____

_____

_____

_____

Understanding Responsibility

Responsibility is about learning what is yours to take, and owning it. It's also about knowing what is not yours, and letting that go. Think of a time when you felt responsible for something that you didn't actually have control over. Maybe you took the blame for an item that broke or went missing—something that you had nothing to do with—just to ease the tension. Perhaps you felt a little responsible for your parents separating. Picture that scenario in your mind, noticing what it feels like in your body. What emotions come up? What is the quality of your thoughts—loud, wild, judging?

Now think of a time when you owned up to a mistake you made. Maybe you accidentally let a private piece of information slip, or you forgot to do a chore around the house. Imagine yourself recognizing your mistake and owning it out loud to others. What does this feel like in your body? What emotions do you notice now? How about the quality of your thoughts?

When we take responsibility for what is ours, we often experience a sense of power—or, at the very least, a little relief. When we try to take responsibility for things that are not ours, or we try to get out of being responsible for something that is, our body knows something is wrong. We'll often get flooded with emotions of helplessness, anxiety, despair, or guilt. Often our minds turn to negative self-talk. When you find yourself in a difficult interaction with someone else, try asking yourself, *What is my responsibility? What is theirs?* See if you can let go of what isn't yours, and own what is.

You are not responsible for how successful your family is in coming together. Sometimes families come together with ease and fun. Other times it can feel clunky, awkward, and upsetting. What three things do you wish your parents would take responsibility for?

Example: I wish my parents would have consistent expectations between them.

1. _____

2. _____

3. _____

How does it feel to know these things are not your responsibility? How could you let them go? (For example, you can write each of them on a separate piece of paper and tear them up, or write them on toilet paper and flush them away.)

_____

_____

_____

_____

_____

_____

With pressures coming from every direction—school, friends, family, and self—it can be hard to be our real selves. What is one way you can promise yourself you will stay true to you, regardless of the feedback you receive from elsewhere? If you need ideas, refer to your description of yourself at the beginning of section 3.

_____

_____

_____

_____

_____

_____

_____

_____

_____

_____

_____

_____

One of the only constant things in life is change. We know it to be true, and yet when change happens in our lives, we often resist it. What is one change in your family that you feel yourself still resisting?

_____

_____

_____

_____

What is one thing you know is always changing but brings you some peace to think about? It could be the seasons, a new day, or even growing up.

_____

_____

_____

_____

How might you use the thought of this peaceful change to help you when you're feeling resistant to change in your family or life?

_____

_____

_____

_____

Reflect On Your Path

Take a moment to reflect on how far you've come throughout your journey. Sit in a comfortable position with a straight back, and let your body settle and rest, noticing where your body makes contact with your seat. Take a few deep breaths and ask yourself, "What has it been like for me to have so much change in my family?" Listen with a soft, affectionate tone. If any physical sensations come up, you can rest your hand gently on that part of your body. Next ask yourself, "What do I still need?" Write down any needs that remain.

_____

_____

_____

_____

_____

_____

_____

_____

_____

_____

Reflect on what you'd hoped to gain from working through this journal. How did it go? What did you accomplish that you'd hoped to, and what do you still need to work on?

_____

_____

_____

_____

_____

_____

If you could take away only one thing you learned or gained from doing this journal, what would it be? What are you taking with you?

_____

_____

_____

_____

_____

_____

Calming Box

As you move forward in your process, sometimes you'll get stuck. You may feel yourself falling into old protective patterns, like shutting down and not speaking your truth. Let's create a toolbox of things you can use to remind yourself of all your progress. Write down ideas you have that might help you snap out of a negative mental state. For example, take a shower, run around the house, or give yourself an affirmation that you learned in this journal. If any of them require additional tools (maybe you listed blowing bubbles, reading a favorite book, or playing a game of cards with your family), find a box and collect the items you'll need so they're ready to go when the time comes.

_____

_____

_____

_____

_____

_____

_____

_____

_____

_____

_____

Name three ways you've seen yourself grow over the past year.

1. _____

2. _____

3. _____

How might you embrace that growth? (Examples are noticing it more in the moment, having a small celebration, or giving yourself more regular high fives.)

_____
_____
_____
_____
_____
_____
_____
_____
_____
_____

Feel Your Power

Learning how to live within your blended family won't always be easy. Remember you are strong, smart, and powerful. Let's try a few exercises to remind you.

1. If you can, stand up and flex your muscles. Or simply pick one muscle to flex—even muscles in your face work. Feel the strength. You can flex and release a few times to feel those muscles working. Notice what they feel like when you're using them.

2. Say your phone number or address backward, out loud. Can you feel your brain working? Your brain can do hard things, even if imperfectly. Flex that brain.

3. Focus on your goal and give it your best effort. You can do it.

4. Write down an example of a time you've been emotionally powerful. Perhaps you supported a friend in need, stood up to a bully, or allowed yourself to cry in front of someone.

You are capable. And your family is lucky to have you.

_____

_____

_____

_____

_____

I AM STRONGER THAN ANY STRUGGLE.

A FINAL WORD

You made it! Look at all the hard work you've put into this journal. You made the choice to bravely explore your feelings and your relationships. Feeling your feelings is no easy task. And you did it. Nice work!

When your family changes and moves away from what you thought you were supposed to have, it's normal to feel a little uncertain at first. It can bring up questions about your place in the family, a sense of loss about what it "should have been," and hesitancy about how to move forward. Change makes us look at ourselves and our lives in new ways. Sometimes it is painful and difficult, and other times it opens us in ways we wouldn't have expected.

Regardless of how your family came to this place, they're here. Your family, blended and all, is what is true in your life. You are not responsible for how successful your family is in coming together—and you still have power over your own thoughts, feelings, and actions. Owning your responsibility in your relationships will help you harness your power. Use that power for good. Find small ways each day to lean into your family in a loving way. Stay honest and kind with your needs, your emotions, and your imperfections (and those of your family). Perhaps one day this change within your family will end up being one of the greatest things to have happened in your life.

My hope is you can find peace in your blended family. I hope you can continue on your journey to seeing and honoring your experience, and acting from your wise place. The better you learn to relate to yourself and your emotions, the easier it will be to engage with your family in healthy ways. Love has no limits, and you are capable of finding joy in your life, exactly the way it is today.

RESOURCES

Mindfulness Apps

Balance—This mindfulness app allows you to choose the voice of your guided meditations. It supports sleep and helps with issues such as fear and pain.

Calm—This mindfulness app offers programs to help you learn and practice meditation. It also has relaxing music, new daily meditations, and stories to lull you to sleep.

Headspace—This mindfulness app is often offered through work and school. It provides customized meditations, help with sleep, and group meditations.

Smiling Mind—This free app walks you through all the steps of learning how to meditate.

Stop, Breathe & Think—This mindfulness app has you first check in about how you're feeling emotionally and physically. Based on your check-in, it offers meditations to support your needs.

Apps to Help Manage Stress

Calm Harm—This is a private, free app for those moments when emotions get overwhelming and self-harming thoughts come. It offers countless activities and ideas to help ride the waves of emotion.

Clear Fear—Similar to Calm Harm and Combined Minds (noted next), this free app is aimed at supporting people through fear and anxiety by using cognitive behavioral therapy (CBT) techniques.

Combined Minds—This is a free app for friends and family to support teens who struggle with anxiety, depression, and other mental health issues.

Cove—This free soothing app allows users to create music to fit their mood.

MindShift CBT—This app tracks your mood, helps you find the right coping skills, and uses CBT to reduce anxiety.

REFERENCES

Miller, W. R. J. C'de Baca, D. B. Matthews, and P. L. Wilbourne. "Personal Values Card Sort." Motivational Interviewing Network of Trainers (MINT). Accessed June 24, 2021. MotivationalInterviewing.org /personal-values-card-sort.

Nagoski, Emily, and Amelia Nagoski. *Burnout: the Secret to Unlocking the Stress Cycle*. New York: Ballantine Books, 2020.

Neff, Kristin. *Self-Compassion*. London: Hodder & Stoughton, 2013.

Ponlop, Dzogchen. *Emotional Rescue: How to Work with Your Emotions to Transform Hurt and Confusion into Energy That Empowers You*. New York: TarcherPerigee, 2017.

Real, Terry, and Juliane Taylor Shore. "The Relational Brain: The Neurobiology of Relational Life Therapy & How It Works to Rewire Your Brain." Relational-brain.com.

Shore, Juliane Taylor. "The Neurobiology of Feeling Safe Working with Boundaries Inside and Out." Academy of Therapy Wisdom. Accessed June 24, 2021. TherapyWisdom.com/neurobiology-of-feeling-safe.

Siegel, Daniel J. *Mindsight: The New Science of Personal Transformation*. New York: Bantam Books, 2010.

ACKNOWLEDGMENTS

The opportunity to put together this journal has been a gift. It could not have happened without the blended family who raised me and supported me through my own journey, and the blended family I've co-created with my husband, who continue to show me the way. I owe a thank-you to my tribe of women, who remind me of how strong we all are. As always, I am infinitely grateful to Callisto Media and the team that supported me, including my editor, Brian Sweeting, in bringing this much-needed journal into the world.

To the many teenage clients I have worked with over the past decade, who always teach me more about the world and remind me of the endless potential for love and growth, thank you.

ABOUT THE AUTHOR

With more than a decade of experience, **Danielle Schlagel** is a Licensed Professional Counselor, Licensed Addictions Counselor, Approved Clinical Supervisor, and a Registered Play Therapist-Supervisor. She is the owner and primary therapist of the group practice at Seity.org. She not only comes from blended families, but has also worked with families and teens from around the world, including blended families of all shapes and sizes. Danielle writes with warmth and honesty, and she firmly believes in being willing to practice all that she preaches. She and her husband blend their family together in Northern Colorado.

CPSIA information can be obtained
at www.ICGtesting.com
Printed in the USA
JSHW011927051021
19325JS00001B/1